THIS IS KOLBY, HE IS GOING TO HELP HIS FAMILY BUY A HOUSE!

KOLBY LIVES WITH HIS MOTHER, FATHER, AND TWO BROTHERS. THEY LIVE IN AN APARTMENT. BUT APARTMENTS CAN BE TOO CONFINING SOMETIMES KOLBY FEELS LIKE THEY ARE ON TOP OF EACH OTHER.

KOLBY'S DAD WORRIES ABOUT HIS FAMILY'S FINANCES. HE WORKS HARD TO MAKE ENDS MEET, BUT STILL CANNOT SEEM TO SAVE ENOUGH MONEY. PLUS, HE'S NOT SURE HOW MUCH MONEY HE NEEDS. HE WANTS TO BUY HIS FAMILY A HOUSE BECAUSE THEY'VE OUTGROWN THEIR SMALL APARTMENT.

ONCE UPON A TIME, THERE WERE ONLY THREE SMARTS: KOLBY, MOM, AND DAD. KOLBY HAD HIS OWN ROOM. HE COULD DO WHATEVER HE WANTED. HIS MOM AND DAD TOOK REALLY GOOD CARE OF HIM. THEY LAUGHED AND TOOK VACATIONS.

BUT SOON THE FAMILY GREW FROM THREE TO FIVE. KOLBY NOW HAS TWO BROTHERS, AND THEY LOVE TO PLAY!

THEY ALSO LOVE TO FIGHT!

THEY PLAY SO MUCH, THEY DON'T DO ANY CHORES. KOLBY'S MOM IS ALWAYS REMINDING THE BOYS TO CLEAN THEIR ROOM.

I'm the
BIG
brother

Kolby's room is really crowded. Instead of one bed, his mom and dad have added two more but he is the big brother.

And he loves his Family.
IF only he had his own room, he would be happy again.
He has a plan....

Kolby suggests his family start a budget to save for a house.

Mom and Dad call a realtor to find out what it takes to purchase a house.

The Realtor drives them around and shows them several houses, then he suggests they call a lender to obtain a mortgage.

The lender asks if they have money saved for a down payment and if they know their credit? Mom and Dad both have a 750-credit score, no worries here!

Dad says they have money in savings, and both have a 401K retirement plan they can borrow from. The lender explains how to calculate how much money they need. Here's the calculation:
Let's say the house costs $200,000.00, the lender will request at least 3.5% for your down payment.

Then, the lender needs to know how much money your mom and dad make a month. This is called the Gross Monthly Income. Next, we look at mom and dad's debts (monthly payments from the credit report).

$3500
$3500
———————
$7000

Mom makes $3500.00 a month and Dad makes $3500.00 a month. Combined, they make $7000.00 a month, that is the gross monthly income. Kolby quickly does the math, Yes, I agree, that is correct!

$85.00

$250.00

$75.00

$125.00

On to debt. Let's say the car is $250.00 a month, $75.00 a month for credit cards, and $125.00 a month for your brothers' new bunkbeds. But last month, Dad bought a new computer for the house, and that payment is $85.00 a month. Let's do the math: $250+$75+125+$85=$535
Wow! a lot of numbers go into buying a house!

There's more! We take $7000.00 (the gross monthly income) and multiply it by 31%. The lenders use this number to determine how much of the $7000.00 can be used for a monthly mortgage payment.

$7000.00x31%=$2170.00 is the monthly mortgage payment.
The lender adds $2170.00 plus $535.00 to get the total amount of debt. This amount is $2705.00.
Lastly, the lender takes $2705 and divides it by $7000.00.
$2705/$7000=38% This is what we call the Debt-to-Income Ratio. It should be below 45%.

I love math!
Congratulations, your debt is in good shape!

Mom and Dad don't want to use their 401K retirement, but their savings are short by $2500.00. How can they raise the additional money needed?
Kolby suggests several ways.

How about a Fundraiser?

Dad and brother help around the neighborhood.

COOKIES

Kolby agrees to bake cookies and sell them at school.

Mom and brother do a neighborhood Dog Wash.

The Smart Family is really smart! They know how much money they need to buy a house. They are sticking to their budget and working extra jobs to make more money. The whole Family works together.

His friends offer their talents too!

Kolby still dreams of the day he gets his own room.
The Smart Family is well on its way to purchasing a new home.

Buying a house doesn't have to be a dream if you plan! Save, budget, and know your numbers like Kolby!

www.ingramcontent.com/pod-product-compliance
Lightning Source LLC
Chambersburg PA
CBHW042027090426
42811CB00016B/1769